Chapter 1

In the early hours of the morning, a section of the new railway line was finally completed. Now it had to be tested. Beneath a full moon, the bright metal of the track stretched into the distance. A steam engine hissed impatiently, as it waited in clouds of twisting smoke. The 'navvies' – men who had built the railway – lined the embankments on either side of the track. Some lay sleeping. Others played cards or dice. Hardly anyone bothered to watch as the train blew its whistle and began to move.

The steam engine picked up speed. The engine's cabin was hot, noisy and cramped. The sweating faces of the driver and the fireman glistened in the fierce heat from the coal fire in the firebox. Both men worked tirelessly to keep the boiler at full pressure. It was dirty, exhausting work.

A third man stood behind, watching them. Wearing a smart dark suit, he looked out of place in the sooty cab.

"'Tis an honour to have you aboard, Sir," shouted the driver above the din. He winked at the fireman. "Who'd have thought it, Fred? Sir Robert, the engineer, in our cab!"

The man in the dark suit smiled. "Well, I couldn't have you men test the new railway bridge on your own," he laughed. "After all, I designed the thing. I should prove it's safe by being the first over it!"

TIME CHRONICLES

Making a Bolt For It

Written by David Hunt
and illustrated by Alex Brychta

OXFORD
UNIVERSITY PRESS

The steam engine chugged on through the moonlit countryside. Sir Robert gazed out as they flashed past countless hedge-lined fields of crops, then cows, then sheep.

"Just round the next bend, and we'll be on your new bridge!" shouted the driver.

Sir Robert smiled to himself. This was an exciting time to be alive. The country was changing, improving, and he was playing a big part in making it happen.

Sir Robert leaned out of the cab to watch the bridge come into view. But something caught his eye as the train steamed on. He thought he saw sheep running alongside the track, past the train ...

Animals don't run towards trains, do they?

At that same moment, the driver called out in alarm. "Look out! Near the bridge! Men, on the tracks!"

With a long blast of the engine's whistle, everyone in the cabin was thrown forwards as the driver pulled the emergency brake.

With its brakes grinding, the steam engine hurtled on towards the bridge. Despite the terrible sound, most of the sheep did not move – caught between the fear of the train, and the fear of something else beyond them. What were those two dark figures doing on the bridge? They seemed to be unscrewing something.

At the last moment, they leapt to one side. At once the sheep scattered out of the way.

For a split second, the men in the cabin felt a great sense of relief. But as the braking engine moved on to the bridge, they were soon gripped by a new horror. To the sound of sickening metallic cracks, the bridge began to jolt and lurch beneath them.

Even in their panic, they sensed what was about to happen. "Go on!" Sir Robert shouted. "The bridge! It's giving way!"

But it was too late. With a deafening crack, a section of the bridge collapsed. The steam engine plunged into the river below.

Chapter 2

Bridge after bridge collapsed. Train after train plunged into the raging current. Fire after fire swamped by freezing water. Metal snapping. Bolts breaking ...

Tyler suddenly woke with a jolt. He rubbed his face. "What a terrible nightmare," he shuddered. "Falling asleep at Control. That's not good." Chewing a pencil to keep himself awake, he stared at the TimeWeb.

Suddenly the pencil dropped from his mouth. Without looking, he hit the alarm. He had seen something terrible.

Whilst Tyler had slept, the Virans had made their move. Tyler was distraught. "I'm so sorry. I must have nodded off."

Mortlock and the others studied the TimeWeb carefully. A black patch had spread its deadly darkness along the Web's fine threads. "This is not good," murmured Mortlock. "The darkness is spreading. It means the initial attack has already succeeded."

"Can we stop it?" asked Chip.

Mortlock looked worried. "If a Viran attack succeeds, then history is changed forever. The changes become what actually happened. They become history. And that has a knock-on effect for every moment that follows, right up to the present. Everything changes. That's why the darkness is beginning to spread up the TimeWeb."

"So we're too late?" said Biff.

"Possibly," nodded Mortlock, grimly.

"Or possibly not!" said Chip. "Look, if it's only just happened, maybe the change won't have had time to spread far yet ..."

Wilma interrupted him. "Yes! If Tyler could send us back to the point where the Viran attack happened, maybe we could change things back again before they take hold."

Mortlock looked uncertain. "Well, it's worth a try. Can you do it, Tyler?"

But Tyler was already at work. "1849. England. I'll get you as close as I can!"

Chapter 3

"Look out!" shouted Chip, as they stepped from the portal. With a rush of choking smoke and swirling sparks, the steam engine slid past Wilma, Chip and Kipper. Tyler had got them close all right – a bit too close.

"What was that?" shouted Kipper.

Chip peered through the smoke. "I can't see. But it's a steam engine, I think."

Seconds later, they heard the sickening crack of shattering metal, and a gigantic crash as the bridge and the engine fell into the river below.

By the time Chip, Kipper and Wilma got to the bridge, it was all over. It was strange to see the way the broken track hung over the edge of a huge gap where a section of the bridge used to be. Chip peered down at the river below.

"There may be men trapped down there!" he shouted. "We have to save them!"

"Chip! Wait!" Wilma was holding her Link. Tyler had sent a download.

But the download wasn't from Tyler.

DOWNLOAD FROM MORTLOCK

This is Mortlock. We can see the bridge in the globe. There is nothing you can do. It's too late. You are not to go near the water. That is an order. T.M.

"Mortlock did say it was probably too late to do anything," said Kipper, quietly.

"But we have to do *something*!" said Chip.

"Maybe," said Wilma. "Look!"

Back down the track, two dark figures were running into the distance.

Chapter 4

"Virans!" hissed Wilma. "Come on!"

"But what about Mortlock's orders?" Kipper called after her.

"Did he say we couldn't catch Virans?" she replied.

Some way down the line, the Virans seemed to be looking for something. Then they dashed up the bank at the side of the track and out of view. Unknown to the Time Runners, the Virans had just located the place where their 'infector' would appear.

Like the Time Runners' portal, an infector enabled the Virans to move through time. Once inside the infector, the Virans' mission would be complete.

The two Virans stood in a field, waiting for the infector to appear. "Any moment we will be gone," sneered one of them. "But our work will remain. Time will set, as hard as stone. It will be impossible for the Time Runners to change it back. Our work here will become history – a history where mankind begins to lose faith in the Industrial Revolution! Progress turned backwards. A change for the worse!"

Following the Virans, Kipper, Chip and Wilma were faced with a terrifying sight at the top of the bank. A black swirling star – the infector – had punched a hole into the air above the two Virans.

Instantly the black star seemed to snatch trails of dark raw energy from one of the Virans.

As his energy blended with the black star's, the Viran's human disguise crumbled into dust.

More out of fear than anything, Wilma launched her Zaptrap. Attracted to the dark energy, it zipped straight towards the infector. For a few seconds, the Zaptrap began to draw dark energy back out of the black star. It was as if the infector and the Zaptrap were locked in a struggle over the Viran's energy. After a moment the Zaptrap snapped shut and fell to the ground, trapping the Viran inside.

Because the infector had been disturbed, it instantly vanished. At this, the remaining Viran let out a piercing snarl. Chip reached for his Zaptrap, but at once the Viran pulled something from his pocket and threw it. Whatever it was, it thumped heavily into Chip's chest, knocking him to the ground. The Viran turned and fled across the field towards a distant hedgerow.

"I'm okay," wheezed Chip, as he pulled himself up. "What hit me?"

"This," said Kipper. He was holding a large iron bolt. It was as big as his hand.

"Maybe it has something to do with what happened at the bridge?" said Wilma. She looked at Chip, who was rubbing his chest. "You need to catch your breath, Chip. Get Tyler to send a portal. Show Mortlock the bolt ... Take the full Zaptrap back too."

"What'll you do?" asked Chip.

"We'll go after the Viran," she said, picking up Chip's Zaptrap. "You up for it, Kipper?"

"You bet," he replied. "Let's go."

Chapter 5

The Viran crossed the field in seconds. Wilma and Kipper saw him reach a dirt road beyond. Some wagons were waiting there for the day's work to begin. They were used to deliver parts to the railway. The Viran leapt on to one of the waiting wagons and drove the horse forward fast along the dirt track. "We mustn't lose sight of him," shouted Wilma.

They set off after him in one of the other wagons. "I can't see him any more," yelled Kipper. "We have to go faster!"

"I can't!" snapped Wilma. "The road
is terrible."

It was true. Wilma was doing her best. But
the wagon was being thrown all over the
place as the horse stumbled over the many
rocks, ruts and potholes.

Around the next bend they suddenly
caught up with the Viran. He had driven
the horse so fast that he had lost control.

The wagon hit a large rock and one of its wheels collapsed. The horse broke free.

The wagon ended up in a ditch. The Viran lay still in the road. A metal bolt lay by his side.

"Now what?" asked Kipper nervously.

Wilma took a step towards the Viran.

"Is he ...?" whispered Kipper.

Suddenly the Viran's eyes snapped open.

His hand closed round the bolt. With the speed of a striking snake, he grabbed at Wilma. She leapt backwards.

Kipper's Zaptrap spun in a comet of sparks toward the Viran. But the Viran was ready. He threw the bolt at the spinning Zaptrap. Instantly, the bolt shattered like glass as the broken Zaptrap fell to the ground. For a second everyone stopped still in disbelief. Then the Viran began to laugh, as he turned and ran.

Chapter 6

Back at the Time Vault, Chip sat in the laboratory, watching Mortlock at work. Mortlock had been studying the bolt Chip had brought back. He had run various tests, and now he sat staring at a piece of the bolt through a microscope. "As I suspected," he suddenly muttered.

He looked up from the microscope and pressed a button to speak to Control. "Tyler, go to the library and find blueprints for all engineering designs around 1849.

We need to see where bolts like these were used on bridges."

"On to it!" came Tyler's reply.

"What is it?" asked Chip.

Mortlock picked up the bolt. "This bolt is very weak. Brittle. Something must have been added to the iron when the bolt was made. The metal is impure." He looked at Chip. "I think I have a plan. But we're going to have to work fast. The history of the Industrial Revolution may depend on it."

Chapter 7

The Viran scrambled down a steep bank on to a path alongside a canal. Kipper and Wilma quickly followed. A little way along, the canal ran into a dark narrow tunnel cut into the side of a hill. Up the side of the hill, the path became a steep flight of steps. At the mouth of the tunnel a coal barge was tied up. It was waiting to be taken through the tunnel.

"We'll catch him at the steps!" shouted Kipper, as they slid down the canal bank after him.

But Kipper was wrong. The Viran didn't take the steps. Instead he leapt on to the barge, scrambled across the coal and dived into the canal at the mouth of the tunnel.

"What now?" said Kipper.

"The barge! Jump in!" Wilma quickly untied the ropes and pushed the barge out into the canal.

The barge slowly drifted into the narrow, damp tunnel. The distant sounds of the Viran in the water echoed through the darkness, fading with every moment that passed.

"Hasn't this barge got an engine or something?" asked Kipper. "I could walk faster than this!"

"An engine! Walk! Of course!" said Wilma. "Kipper, get on your back, put your feet on the roof of the tunnel, and walk!"

It was hard, dirty work. The tunnel seemed to go on forever. But despite all their efforts they couldn't keep up. The sound of the Viran had disappeared some time before they saw light at the end of the tunnel.

But when they finally emerged into the dawn of a new day they were greeted with a sight that took their breath away. They had arrived right into the middle of a busy, smoky industrial town.

Chapter 8

The blueprint design of Sir Robert's bridge was stretched out on the table in the library. "If you look closely, you'll see the bolt was used to attach the girders to the upright trusses," said Tyler.

"So the bolts would have to be strong enough to take both the weight of the bridge, and anything crossing it," said Chip.

"Correct!" said Mortlock, who had just come back from his workshop. "The bolt Chip brought back was not able to cope with the stress that it was put under."

"But what can we do?" asked Chip. "The Virans have beaten us on this one."

"There may be a way," said Mortlock. He put a bag of bolts on the table. "I've made these in the workshop. They are identical, except that the iron is good. It's not brittle. If we could somehow replace the Viran bolts just before the train crosses ..."

"But what about the Virans?" asked Chip. "Won't they still be there?"

"Yes. No, well, possibly. The plan ... It all depends on whether Wilma and Kipper can catch the other Viran."

Chapter 9

"We'll never catch the Viran now," said Wilma. "He'll be miles away." They tied the coal barge alongside a number of others waiting to unload at a cotton mill.

In actual fact they were closer to the Viran than they thought. Much closer. Four barges along, the Viran had been hiding after his long swim. At the sound of their voices, he leapt from the barge, ran across the cobbled quayside and into the mill. "After him!" shouted Kipper. "He's gone up the stairs."

In the mill, an extraordinary sight greeted Wilma and Kipper as they entered the vast machine room at the top of the stairs. The Viran had been caught!

Pushing past the terrified mill-workers, he had nearly made it to an open door at the other end of the room. But his arm had caught one of the cotton-spinning machines. Like a strange fly caught in a web, the more he struggled, the more he became entangled.

Kipper shouted the first thing that came into his head. "Stop that man! He's a thief!"

Not knowing what they were dealing with, a few of the workers stepped towards the snarling Viran. Immediately, he filled the air around him with a choking Viran darkness.

"Smoke!" a worker screamed. "The machine's on fire!"

In a panic, the workers ran towards Wilma and Kipper, pushing them back to the door.

"Under the machines!" shouted Wilma. "Crawl! It's the only way we'll get to him!"

It was a race. Beneath rows of dangerous machinery, Wilma and Kipper crawled towards the Viran as he struggled to free himself.

But they were not even close when the Viran finally broke free. He laughed as he stepped towards the open door.

Hanging above the door was a rope and pulley used to pull up bundles of raw cotton. He grabbed the rope and swung out. But by now, there were no workers to get in the way. Kipper rolled out from under a machine, stood up, and launched his Zaptrap as hard as he could.

Chapter 10

Tyler had sent Chip back again to just before the train crash. In a field of sheep, he waited. He could see the bridge. He had a bag full of the replacement bolts Mortlock had made. Chip understood that bit of Mortlock's plan. But as for the rest of it ... Mortlock had told him to take his Zaptrap – with the Viran he had caught still in it! And what Chip really couldn't get his head around was that he knew the very same Viran was, at that moment, also down on the bridge, carrying out his deadly work.

What is more, Mortlock's plan would only work if both Virans were captured and brought back to where Chip was. That depended on Wilma and Kipper.

The sound of a train's whistle broke the silence. Chip spoke to Tyler.

"We've heard nothing yet," came Tyler's reply. "But I'll divert the portal so they come straight to you from where they are."

Chip could now hear the distant sound of the train chugging down the track. He had to do something, but what?

With a vague plan that he might somehow stop the train before it got to the bridge, Chip ran across the field. Sheep scattered ahead of him. Sheep! That was it!

Chip desperately stumbled about, trying to drive as many sheep on to the track as possible.

The sound of the train grew louder. The sheep would slow the train down, but not for long, and they wouldn't stop the Virans.

Then, to his relief, a familiar glowing door appeared between him and the bridge.

Moments later, Chip, Wilma and Kipper were racing towards the bridge clutching both Zaptraps. "Do exactly as I do!" Chip shouted as they ran.

At the sight of the Virans, Chip and then Kipper pressed the release buttons on

their Zaptraps before dropping them on the ground. Instantly, the energy from both freed Virans hissed from the open Zaptraps. The Virans on the bridge had barely a moment to scream. Their dark energy was sucked from their human disguise, smashing into the energy released from the Zaptraps. For a moment nature itself seemed to shriek in terrible pain as the energy collided together.

Now Chip understood the rest of Mortlock's plan. It was not possible for two versions of the same thing to exist in the same moment. The Virans had cancelled themselves out in a terrible storm of energy.

It was over. Or was it? "Quickly!" Chip shouted. With the bolts in hand, they frantically undid the Virans' work, as the sound of the distant train grew louder. The last bolt was in place just as the wheels of the engine carrying Sir Robert and the men crossed on to the bridge.

They lay on the ground, exhausted. Chip felt sure he could just make out the sound of the men cheering as the engine travelled onwards beyond the bridge. "History, back on track!" he sighed.

Glossary

blueprints *(page 27)* A detailed drawing or design, used as a plan to work out how something could be built. *"Tyler, go to the library and find blueprints for all engineering designs around 1849."*

embankment *(page 3)* A raised bank of earth, built to carry a railway. The 'navvies' – men who had built the railway – lined the embankments on either side of the track.

girders *(page 33)* Metal beams used to help support the weight of a structure such as a bridge. *"If you look closely, you'll see the bolt was used to attach the girders to the upright 'trusses.'"*

impure *(page 28)* Mixed with unwanted substances. *"Something must have been added to the iron when the bolt was made. The metal was impure."*

trusses *(page 33)* Vertical metal frames used to support the length of a structure. *"If you look closely, you'll see the bolt was used to attach the girders to the upright 'trusses.'"*

Thesaurus: Another word for ...

impure *(page 28)* corrupted, tainted, contaminated.

Mortlock's Mission Report

Location: *England*

Date: *1849*

Mission Status: *Successful*

Notes: *Since I was directly involved in this mission, I have asked Tyler if I might write the end files on this one. I am particularly pleased since I hold the Industrial Revolution in great awe.*

The curiosity of the human mind – that is what I find so fascinating about the Industrial Revolution. Here was a time where ideas fed other ideas. But it wasn't just a case of one idea following on from another. One idea might spark off any number of other ideas in every direction, in every aspect of life. Change was everywhere.

But these ideas were not only communicated through words. This was a new language. This was the language of machines. And if machines were the language, then iron was its vocabulary. Iron. Mix iron ore, charcoal, limestone. Add heat and oxygen. Get the mix right, and you produce a substance with which you can build a machine. With a machine, you can build a revolution.

T.M.

History: downloaded!
The Industrial Revolution

People have always tried to use the world around them to their advantage. Humans have always had the impulse to pick up something, such as a stone, turn it in their hands and think, 'I can make something with this!' Up until the Industrial Revolution, the big shifts in history were about changes in the way people understood the world around them, and the way they worked with the opportunities that nature presented.

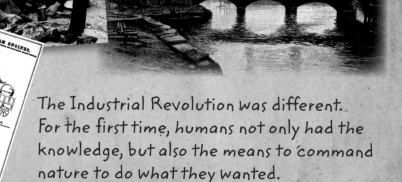

The Industrial Revolution was different. For the first time, humans not only had the knowledge, but also the means to command nature to do what they wanted.

After the Industrial Revolution, farming no longer relied entirely on the natural rhythms. More food was produced from larger fields, with new machinery and fertilizers.

With the burning of coal, a massive amount of energy could be harnessed to power machinery. Railways could take people further and faster than ever before.

By building canals, people could divert water to where they needed it to go.

Steam power replaced sail, enabling trade between countries to increase.

Even people's role in the natural world changed. They no longer relied only on the land, as increasing numbers worked in factories operating machines that did many times more work than a human could do.

For more information, see the Time Chronicles website:
www.oxfordprimary.co.uk/timechronicles

A voice from history

These machines I tend. 'Mules', they call them. They spin cotton fibres into thread. I mind the mules with my two 'piecers'. Young 'uns they are. Nip under the mule to piece together any threads that snap. It's dangerous work. You have to be little, and quick, else you get caught by the machine.

Fifteen hours a day we do this, in a huge room full of mules. Deafening noise. The air is hot and damp, filled with cotton fluff, blizzarding about like snow. Choking our lungs.

I'm told one mule does the work of near twenty people. And I mind four of 'em. I ask myself, how long before the machines don't even need me anymore? A mule! We're the ones treated like a worthless animal. It's the machine that matters.